MW01173940

MUSINGS OF
AN ISLAND GIRL

there it is again.

that churning,
burning,
yearning;
that overwhelming desire to yell
the things that are bubbling up inside me
but i cannot find my voice
so these stories i cannot tell.

MUSINGS OF
AN ISLAND GIRL
By Emme Howitt

Copyright © 2024 Emme Howitt

All rights reserved.

No part of this publication may be reproduced without the author's consent.

Photo credits:

Cover: EyeEm Mobile GmbH

Wilfried Wende (7), Photo Concepts(8), Roman Kraft (23), David McElwee (52), Engina Kyurt (61), Jill Wellington (65), Matteo Catanese (69), Jagjit Singh (79), Jeffersn Santos (82), Rohul Pandit (85), Marlona Beltran (87)

ISBN: 9798339277255

Dedicated to my Mother, Thelma. You never left any stone unturned.

This is for that woman or that girl who has been silently, patiently waiting and working for her day. That woman, that girl who has borne everything that has been thrown her way but has not lost sight of herself. It is for that woman, that girl who has withstood and is still determined to make her mark.

Against all odds, she has raised herself up; the waters and the muck have washed over her, but she has not been soiled. She has defied the challenges, the restrictions, the dividing lines, the coffin boxes, she has broken the ropes on her hands, the chains on her feet, she has stepped out of the mold.

She imagines her worth and she is determined to prove it. She will accept nothing less. She is a force of nature, a restless ocean, a hunting tigress, a ravenous wind!

It is for me, and for my island, Jamaica, rising up above the odds of 'colonization', breaking chains, breaking barriers, wriggling out of the cocoon of other people's expectations to *fly* and *fly* and *fly*!

MY CHILDHOOD WAS DIFFICULT BUT
BEAUTIFUL
BECAUSE THERE WAS ALWAYS ENOUGH
SOFT GRASS
TO COVER THE ROCKS
AND THE BUTTERFLIES ALWAYS CAME
OUT AFTER THE RAIN!

Red Watering Can

Little girl dreams,
swishing, swishing, swishing
inside tiny hands
holding on tightly to her prized watering
can,
with the pretty yellow daisies and the little
dream girl,
turned into real girl-
friend helping to keep
the pretty pink periwinkle smiling at the
bobbing butterflies.
Red watering can,
jostling, splish-splashing
little girl dreams in little girl hands,
spilling drops of possibilities
amidst the stony reality.
Little girl hopes
like perfect diamond drops
slipping and sliding
on the soft white petals,
like little girl dreams
baked inside soft white pillows,
floating colourful and carefree
in fleeting night time visions.

Yes

We

Can!

I
want to
make music
with my
words
ra-ta-ta-ta
ta-ta
tam tam
I want
you to
sing
a-ling
and
dance
dance to the sounds
beautiful   sounds of
my song   in your ear;
whisper them to your lover,
Teach them to your children
then dance, dance together
to the music of my words;
feel the rhythm of each line
close your eyes,
come alive
feel the beat (ta-tam) let
the rhythm flow through you
like sweet wine; don't hesitate
just embrace the life pulsing
through your veins through the
words of my song then sing, sing
along. Feel the rhythm purging,
making you freet - ta-dam, ta-dee
you are the rhythm, you are the
beat in this song, sing with me
together we'll make music
Yes we can!

11

Let Them Talk

Hear them talking
Let them talk!
They are talking
They have to talk!

They talk about what they do not
understand
They cannot fathom the uniqueness of
this woman.
They talk about the way I walk, head held
high, chin jutting forward
Eyes set on a target they cannot see;
They talk about my steadfast smile
Never fading though oppression
Sometimes brings me to my knees.

They talk about my steady gait
My unflinching faith
They backbite and slander my name

*Then they talk about how my heart
never breaks.*

Hear them *talking*
Let them talk
They are talking
They have to talk.

They screech like **tormented** birds
Whispering behind my back
Then lying to my face,
But their eyes give them away, yes!
They come to me as friends,
They are wolves dressed up as sheep,
They come to find fuel to feed
Their hunger for **incessant** speech.

They are talking
Hear them talking
They need to talk to feel real
But talk is cheap.

I do not join in their meaningless chatter,
I listen, I learn,
My silence reaches above the din they
create
Frightens them
They do not understand,
They cannot fathom
Someone who does not get fat on gossip,
slander, strife, shame.

Hear them talking
They are *talking*, *talking*, *talking*!
They do not stop to think or to feel
They cannot find time to care.

They cocoon themselves with empty
speech
Hiding from the real world
Their babbling tongues the only thing of
worth they own.
They are the *talkers*,
They must talk
They do not learn
How can they learn?

They have no time to listen
Their ears are numb from the echo of their
own voices
Their tongues are fit as fiddles
But their minds have aged without
maturing.
They throw words like poisoned darts
Striking down who they can,
Stripping Youthfulness from the young
Murdering the aged with their venomous
tongues.

Will their lips ever speak praise?
Will their words ever reach out like
helping hands to lift a sister up?
Will their speech ever flow like healing oil
To soothe the wounds of a brother broken
and torn
By life's cruel hands?

Let them talk if talk is all they can
Let them talk!
They *talk* and *talk* and *talk*
They do not understand

They are the Talkers
They cannot understand the gift of measured speech,
The golden beauty of silent lips
They cannot fathom the beauty of this woman
Moving so quietly in the land,
Oblivious to their spiteful chatter.
They have to talk
So let them talk!

My Beautiful Afro

Said you liked the real Jamaican coffee
 You liked it black
  No cream, no sugar
   But you liked it hot.
    My heart stirred,
     Best pick-up line
      I ever heard
      You spending time with me
       Buying me gifts
        Oh this is bliss!

      It's been a while
       I realize
        You have no family or friends
         Or else, you're keeping me from
them.
    Your lame excuses cannot make amends
      So just be real, please don't pretend.

         Our private world has been upset
        Your family and friends will not accept
          Your cream with my coffee
           Now it's your world or mine
            To choose is to lose
             Yet I must refuse
      No cream will lighten my coffeed skin
       Nor rob my beautiful Afro of its kink

Goodbye
I'll always remember that you tried.
What you are able to see
Is who I am inside
For me to change
would be a lie
So I'll choose to keep my coffee,
My afro and my pride.

That Red Dress

There it was. The one thing I owned all by
myself
It's the one thing I own, just me and
nobody else.
It was not like this house
Filled to the brim with my ma-in-law and
her mouth
Set in a permanent pout
Just ready for fault finding;
Plus my sister-in-law and her husband
and their three
can-do-no-wrong children.
It was not like this room with barely
enough space for air,
Stuffed as it is with all sorts of hand-me-
down furniture
For which I don't really care;
It was not like my one good shoes,
The one single pair
My sister-in-law will not stop borrowing,
Nor like my sister Joy, who won't stop
sorrowing
Over her no good ex who left her over a
year now, and, well who's counting?

It was not like Joe,
The boy I share with my husband Daniel,
Nor like the kind Daniel,
Who still thinks I'm not smart enough to figure out
I've been sharing him since just a few months after our wedding.

It's the one thing I own
That has served me so well,
It's the one thing I own, just me and no one else.
First it took me in fine style to serve as maid-of-honour
to my best friend
Then it took me to Joe's first graduation, and it will take me to the next.
Then I'm saving it for Ma's funeral, no matter what Daniel says,
For I know her pouting lips
For once will not be able to dampen my moment of utter bliss,
Nor will her condescending tone
Make me feel less than anybody else
When I flounce up the aisle
In that red dress.

In The Ghetto

Everyday we talk bout the Ghetto Youth,
Hiding from the truth of who we are.
A ready-made scapegoat, the Ghetto
Youth,
Born to bear the brunt of another man's
wrongs.

How many of us ever been to the Ghetto?
Know if the children really let-go?
Know what them eat?
Why them play in the street?
But everyday we beat down the Ghetto.

Tell me, who created the Ghetto Youth?
Who created the Ghetto?
Who tells them the truth,
Fashions the minds of these youths,
Who tells them they belong to the Ghetto?

How many streets are in the Ghetto?
Where does it end, where does it start,
Who builds zinc fences round our hearts?

How many youths live in the Ghetto?
Who brings the truth to the Ghetto?
Where are the malls, the stalls, the halls?
Where is the life, who start the strife?
Who brings peace to the ghetto?

Who brings them piece of the pie?
Who tells them the vicious lies?
Who is willing to die, who will cry or try
To fight for the night of the Ghetto youth?
Who will fight for the rights of the Ghetto?

Tell me how do you know a Ghetto Youth?
Is it his clothes, the shape of his nose
The things he knows...?

Somebody show me the Ghetto.
Tell me where, how to get there
By car? Is it really far?
Somebody please tell me
Does the Ghetto live inside me or do I
Live in the Ghetto?

Premature

Premature baby
Premature birth
Conceived in a hurry
Born too soon
Premature child
Premature growth
Grew up too fast
Dropped out of school
Premature life
Premature work
Not enough money
Not many moons
Premature existence
Premature death
Died in a hurry
Gone too soon.

Fo my niece, for my brother.

Nine Nights

It's the first night and here they come
Demanding rum
Dominoes beating the hurriedly set out
tables
Like drums.
My heart beats in time but my emotions
are locked in tight,
Reality and fantasy are intertwined.
It's the first night,
A little moisture blurs my sight but
My heart refuses to accept and
The tears refuse to come.

Night two and
I'm feeling blue
I'm beginning to realize
That something is amiss
No more hugs, no kiss –
Your eyes will never again see my faults
Nor will correction
Ever spill from your pouting lips;
Today I cried a little
And hurriedly dried my eyes

Need to set more tables out, and how?
Last night's few have returned bringing others
In tow.

Tees to cross, blanks to fill
The place you occupied is empty still
Unwelcome tasks to perform against my will,
Yet still tonight they come again to ensure
I am wide awake and able to endure
The pain of losing you.
Sleep beckons with its anesthetic spell
But so many stories and
So many mouths to tell
From your childhood up until...
They think they knew you so well.

Night four
I have rum and punch –
They have sympathies to pour
My open door reveals all but my broken heart;
Curiosity gets its fill and
Later on more stories will spill –

How many rooms, how many beds
How many pillows were cushioning our
heads
But tonight everyone's a cousin or a friend
Come to keep company at our expense.

Five and four make nine
Why does time linger so when you want it
to fly?
How do others stand the din
It's all I can do to keep my anger in.
Everyone laughing, having fun
While my world hangs upside down;
Curry, scallion, garlic, thyme
Pumpkin, cho-cho, carrot, lime
Goat to kill, more blood to spill
The so-called community must have its
fill.

Six
I'm picking up sticks,
Ram soup to boil, can't let the talk be
That ni'night spoil.
Pepsi for some to mix in with the rum
For others soft drinks or beer –
Brown sugar and lime won't sit well
In the empty spaces senna pod and mojo
herb have cleared
And just as I feared, the numbers keep
increasing.

A perfect number for some, that's seven
I'm thinking of all kinds of things
Like heaven
And when these nights of torture will end.
I'm thinking in bits and pieces
Smiling and greeting friends and relatives
Tonight there are more helping hands
Some pouring in from country
Others trickling in from foreign lands
Didn't realize how long the bloodline was
till now
And how, introductions passing all around
It's at times like this you know your own.

This smile glued to my face
Has lasted till day eight
Will it serve till tomorrow or crack
When this numbness wears off and my
feelings come back
I'm going through the motions like a
puppet on a string
But no amount of string pulling can
Lift your once agile limbs or
Bring you back to the choir to sing
Your envied seat already filled, I bet
Or maybe not yet
If conscience and good sense
Which have failed to show up here
Have chosen instead the church as a
preferred residence.

Why nine?
One, three or five would've been fine.
Maybe nine gives enough time
To remember all the sins
Committed against one's kin—
All the expenses now just a minor thing.
What to compensate for the anger, the
jealousy
The hate, the neglect?
One last night to reminisce
Then tomorrow the bitter bliss
As relief and sadness mix
And finally the tears and scattered roses
will fall
In abundance to relieve the pent-up grief,
The fear and secret relief
It's you, not me that will be missed.

A Way With Words

You have a way with words (my friend)
He said often enough
Till I almost believed it;
It could be true if I cared to think about it.
T'was true if I dared to admit it.
It was true until I laid down burdened in
my bed,
Till I needed a friend
And no word that I had ever said
Urged him to come and visit.

No thought that I had ever shared,
No line that I had ever written
To him at any time or in any season
Gave him sufficient reason
To extend a needed hand.
So for a while I wondered
But no words would come
To soothe the horror of what he had done
Or even to excuse it.

So I lay there by my lonesome self
And thought about the thing he'd said
And thought about the way ahead
Then those thoughts took shape in my
head
And the things my heart could not
comprehend
Turned into words at the tip of my pen
And out poured everything I felt;
I found a way to heal and then
At last I dared to tell myself,
You have a way with words, my friend.
You have a way with words, my friend.

In The Other Jamaica

Round here women are a dime a dozen
And men are scarce as good gold
Not in number, no
For they dominate the streets
And congregate in their masses on the
corner each day
Religious in their ritual worship of the
Weed
And maybe Ras Tafari.

Many of them cannot wash, cook, clean or
tidy themselves
Or balance books, weed grass or paint
fence,
Yet they are great men, tall in stature
Rising and spreading wide as the Blue
Mountains in the East
If you listen to them speak.
Their voices reach up to the skies,
As tall perhaps as their man-made egos
They build castles and live as kings
Drive the fastest cars, have the most girls,
star the most shows –
They run things.

Round here school is a place for the rich
and for fools
And church is a holiday fling
Where would one get money to buy
education,
Or coins to fill up Parson's offering pan?
Round here the children learn from early
on
You don't need money to ghet-to
education
You just need to learn to be or to please a
man
Round here in this other land
In this other Jamaica
Round here where I come from.

Round here two ounce o' salt fish feed a
family of six
Round here hungry bite, life beat and
poverty lick we fo' six
We don't write the script,
We're the actors, we live it
The Merry Mondays, Wacky Wednesdays
And the lively street politricks.

Round here even the youngest youth know
how to make ends meet
Round here you learn from early how to
hustle if you want to eat;
A little hustling each day keep starvation
away
Or sort out your bling bling for Furious
Friday.

Round here little girls trying really hard
not to turn mule
Round here little boys waters trying to
"bun grass" really soon
No problem man,
Round here we make room for every
generation
In numbers we find solace
Round here on our little patch of land.

An island within an island
It's where we come from
We write our own laws
On the doorpost and the lintels and in our
children's hearts

You who don't come from 'round here
You may not understand
This is our Iegacy, we inherit it
We belong to this land.
We too are true Jamaicans
Though we live so differently
We not too far from the other Jamaica,
Just down the lane, round the corner
Round here is where you will find me.

If someone had told me
Maybe I would've thought he had lied.
If someone had warned me,
Maybe I would've said it's still worth a try.
But having done it, felt it, embraced it,
endured it,
I'm asking myself why
Didn't someone tell me,
warn me, try to stop me, deliver me;
Why did no one even try?

The Cinderella in My Story

She dreamed of her prince a very long
time ago
When her world was right side up
When her days were intact
When the nighttime meant that a new day
would be born.
She could dream then, could see visions
She could touch the gold of the sun
And after every rain, a rainbow would
come.

Then she slept on steadfast pillows
Then the darkness could whisper but it
couldn't touch
A girl could dream of sparkly tomorrows
Of white steeds and charming princes
Of pumpkin spiced carriages
She could sip tea with fairy godmothers
And wear the daintiest little sandals.

Way back then a girl could dream all night
uninterrupted
When the stars and the angels kept
company

When a promise made was a promise kept
When a mommy and a dad were the best
of friends
Before the world tripped
Before her dreams flipped
And nightmares became real and living.

She dreamed about him a very, very long
time ago
Way back when a girl's dreams could
breathe without wheezing
When roses and violets were true red and
blue
Back when knights were chivalrous
When forever was a love pact
When one and another were two
And sweet nothings were everything
and true.

~~It's how we raise our sons~~

It's how we raise our sons
How we teach them right, and wrong
How we insist they are strong
Little boy must be big man.

Bad boy
Rude boy
Tough boy
Don't cry boy,
You're a man.

It's how we raise our sons
To leave the beds unspread
Only girls need to be well read
Little boy must be rough, man.

Bad boy
Rude boy
Tough boy
Don't sigh boy,
Be a man.

It's how we raise our sons
Turn the world upside down
You'll do better when you're grown
Little boy must be boy, man.

Bad boy
Rude boy
Tough boy
Don't be shy, boy,
You're a man.

It's how we raise our sons
How we show them right is wrong
What we tell them makes them strong
Little boy must have girls, man.

Bad boy
Rude boy
Tough boy
Sometimes you lie boy,
To be a man.

Heart

bro

ken

This way   and that
This way   and that
You've been   most unkind
Tormenting   my mind
Pulling me   this way
Shoving me   that
Till I'm   hurt
And   broken
And   wishing
You'd
Stop

I Buy Mangoes at the Market

It was my mango tree that I planted,
Right at the side of the house where I
planned to have the garden
But that was before she came along, I
think
Maybe it was before I found out
Now she eats mangoes in the summertime
From the tree that I planted
And I buy mangoes at the market for my
son's.

Sometimes I still remember how I
desperately longed for fruit
And how the sight of the pretty blossoms
gave me hope
But that was early spring
And by summer when the fruits came
I was buying mangoes at the market for
my sons.

Do You Remember,

Hammers and nails.
The cries of a newborn baby and gut –
wrenching pain.
The persistent throbbing in my head,
 My mind desperately trying to form a
rhyme
With words that just would not come out
right.
My heart mimicking the beat of the
hammer on nails
Thump, Thump Thump
The incessant pain,
Searing through my gut (again and again)
Searching for my heart
A heart you should have been protecting
A heart you were so intent on breaking
Time and time again.
Then the hammer and the nails
Beating time to a song with lyrics I could
not understand.

Hammer and nails
It's Sunday morning and gut wrenching
pain,
A scalpel and a needle
With anaesthetic too feeble to relieve
Life's cruel mistakes.
The dance of the scalpel in unskilled
hands and the punishing pain and the soft
cries of a son
Thursday's battle fought and won
Then comes Sunday and the dreadful
drums
With the hammer and nails in a steady
hand;
Though it was not all in vain
Yet the haunting hum of the hammer will
prevail.

Thump Thump Thump
Building a box to store the pain?
Burying us alive again?
Do you still carry the beat in your head
The beat of the hammer and the damning
dread
Did the nail scars imprint on your
hardened heart?

So early on that Sunday morn
With the new babe lying in my arms
You could have been a father
You chose instead
The horrid hammer, Thump! Thump!
The nails, the box of pain,
Undertaker burying my wedding dress and
veil,
My life's work bundled with our son's
games
His childhood boxed in with my fortune
and fame.

I still remember the hammer and the nails
The coffin that took two years to break
The termites eating away your soul
The lies and the pain and games the and
the hate
And your cruel eyes trying to seal my fate.

Let me forget that hammer, those nails,
That box and most of all your face.
Watch me rise from the bed of torturous
hate
To live, to laugh, to soar, to gain

To find myself, to recreate
The dreams I dreamed before you came.
Hammer and nails
Watch me build my life again!

Port Royal,

That's where I saw you for the very first
time
Your manly frame weakened against that
Giant of a lighthouse
Your dark skin and heart incomparable to
its pristine white;
Then I saw its eyes,
Which could search out the darkest night
To find a lost soul yearning for a light;
And I saw you standing there blackhearted
and blind.

I came home sitting beside you
But my heart had left you behind,
Right there in the sand and the spray
of Port Royal
Where I saw you for the very first time
today.

the holes in my soles

I bought darning things again today
I got holes to mend from the wear and the
fray
My fingers, they are nimble in a practiced
sort of way
My ears, they are numb to the damning
things you say.

I got things to darn, you got things to
damn
God writes, you try to erase His Master
Plan
It's you and the devil working hand in
hand
Trying really hard to mash up everybody's
plans.

My ears hear but my heart refuses
Even though sometimes my mind
confuses
Your outstretched hand for an act of
kindness

Then the slap to my face always reminds
me.

I got holes in my soles, I've been running
from trouble,
Wear, tear, your mouth working on the
double
Weaving wickedness in the ordinary
words people say
Me, I'm just singing and darning away.

You break promises, break backs, break
dreams, break hearts,
Your crooked finger poking and tearing
lives apart
You've made destruction your lifelong
mission
Left me with all them holes and twenty-
twenty vision.

I got holes to mend again today
I got some songs to sing and some prayers
to pray
I got a ways to go to get away
Before the hole in my soul decides to stay.

I walk alone,
Not because I have not
Stepped out, reached out,
Denied myself, played dead;

I walk alone
Not because I cannot see
On the contrary,
I clearly see who I need to be.

I walk alone, among the throngs
Extend myself, see where I belong
I open my eyes, I open my mouth
Truth like a flame dances on my tongue;

My heart beats, I'm my own drum
I step to a simple, honest hum,
My footprints pen a timeless song
And I carry my dreams in my own hands;

I walk alone
Not because the streets are empty
But because everyone I meet is a
passerby
And no one dares to walk with me.

I Lived on Anderson Street

I lived on Anderson Street,
Back when the birds were singing new songs
And the roosters crowed at their own will.
When the children knew they were children
When mothers loved their own and everyone else's.
I didn't want to live there then
I went there against my will,
I would have lived almost anywhere else
I lived there until I'd had my fill.

I lived on Anderson Street,
Where children roam the streets without a
scolding
Kneading palms and laughing at their
uniformed friends.
Where the roosters crow when they are
told
Where the birdsongs are melodious but
old,
They have nothing new to tell
They've lived there longer than most
In that earthly hell.

I lived on Anderson Street.
Lived? I can call it that or just about
anything else.
I existed, I survived, I sojourned, I almost
died;
I learned that things are not usually as
they seem,
I learned that all my first impressions
were but dreams.

I lived on Anderson Street,
For years and years till I stopped counting.
Three years he said it would be at most
Somehow I knew that would not be.
I was sentenced mostly to solitary
confinement,
Maximum security with labour that was
always much too hard,
While he roamed wherever he wanted and
was never there to stand guard.

I lived on Anderson Street.
Yes, sixteen years and more, I finally
counted.
I loved, I lost, I fought, I won,
I learned the value of the little I had.
I learned that witches go to church on
Sunday
Dressed in their finest array,
I learned that no one can really defeat you
When you learn to watch and pray.

I lived on Anderson Street,
From the start against my will
Some will expect me to say I'm grateful
For hardships endured and the pain I felt.
I am not! In fact I am only grateful for this
pen,
I am only grateful that I have lived to tell;
I could have lived wherever I wanted
It did not have to be near hell.

This Particular Pile of Refuse

Here lies
All those crinkly see through wrappers
that I wore
Me and the tons of Candys from the store
A cardboard box and really thick white
foam
That carried me safely to our happy home
Maybe every single word you ever said
"Love you", "Baby" and the catchy ones
you'd read
Silly bouquet of paper roses not quite red
Silly dreams made on pillows all now
shred.

Here lies
Hope and Faith and Grace and Trust all
dead
A million things we thought but never said
Swept up bits and pieces from the
hardwood floor
Some still quite fresh and some from days
of yore

Then the cruel thorns and thistles from
your side
That kept poking at my happiness, my
pride
It was as the fire rose the fire died
Could be murder or a selfish suicide.

Musings of an Island Girl

As if it was not enough,
She was left to fend on her own
For herself and children conceived in a
rush
Of love and childish discovery of
adulthood;
A fulfillment of fantasies,
No dream actually being realized,
Except that her glazed over, love-worn
eyes
Created a veil of bliss that did not truly
exist except inside.

Enveloped in his lovely arms
She is wooed and succumbs to his superior
whims
She fancies that the things he says he
means
But he, maybe unable to help himself,
His practiced tongue just a wretched
wielding whip-
An ancestral legacy masquerading
misguided manly myths,
Is in fact just another marauding bandit

Who manacles young girls' minds.

She, having been fatherless,
Having shunned her mothers' wit
She, not desiring to be labeled feminist or
wise,
Chooses instead a path less resistant
Not fully comprehending
That she is just a victim of that inherent in
his genes
Or maybe just his jeans,
And then as if that was not enough,
She gets to watch repeated history with
her girls.

Infallible

I didn't fall,
I landed
I didn't bruise,
I changed my skin
I didn't succumb,
I accepted
I didn't lose,
I let go
I didn't crumble
I extended myself
I didn't give up,
I recreated
I didn't die,
I rested
I didn't stop,
I'm still waiting.

T'was Only Five Little Pebbles

Maybe it was the History
How he knew that lions mouths could be
shut
How bears could be cuddly soft to the
touch
Maybe it was the History, maybe that was
enough.

Maybe it was the Science
How he knew that heavy loads could move
on a tiny pivot
How gravity can surely pull the mighty
down to earth
Maybe it was the Science, maybe that was
enough.

Maybe it was the Math
How he knew that a great sea could be
divided
How he knew that a giant made the
balance lopsided
Maybe it was the Math, maybe that was
enough.

Maybe my History is not worth recording
Maybe my Science is a beaker of failed experiments
Maybe my Math does not add up,
Maybe all I have are five little pebbles
Faith, Love, Hope, Forgiveness and Trust,
and maybe that is enough.

One Mustard Seed

One small pulse, one lucid thought begins
to form
One speck of dust inside a gleam of light,
hope is born –
Out of the nothingness of certain death,
A thought unraveled from the stink of
neglect,
From the bottom of the pit of despair
Where days turned to months turned to
years,
The worms ate, and hope took one last
breath.

Did time stop? Did anyone lament? Did
your sisters have your back, could they
comprehend?
Did they reach down there into your
emptiness
To try to grab at the straws of your
existence?
Did they even understand the depth,
The treachery of every step they would
take

To get to the Faith that could bring you
back to them?

Faith that once stood solitary and still,
In this exact uncompromising state,
Where pain is a real place,
Where deceit and despair unite against
your fate.
In this solitary place, a speck of mustard
seed Faith,
A whispered prayer caught on the wind,
A single need, a desperate lament,
Digging through the ashes of what could
have been
To find one single seed that could recreate
the promise of one's beginning,

And then that single verse, "Come forth!"
And there it was, and
Up from the dust, four days later he came,
Unraveled! Unsoiled! Undead!
Unashamed!
His only claim a subtle revelation of a
truth already known,
A truth to grab and make one's own:

You never die until The Master says "It's done!"

History Lessons

The History of my mothers
Passed down to us on rainy days and long
summer nights
Amidst the smells of boiling coconut and
sugar, and
hallelujah tucked in between two hells,
A bit warmer than our wriggly toes poking
and wrangling for more space
to tuck in ever so tightly under Mama's
worn out sheet,
Our ears and our noses twitching
expectantly,
anticipating the promised treats.

Duppy stories stealthily slipping in from
across the Atlantic
with Anancy and the rest,
And we try to remember how far away the
crossroad is,
Every sound now a threat,
That rolling calf might disregard street
lights and
find a way to unlatch innocent people's
gates,

But the tug of warm cornmeal pudding
and grater cake
keep our eyes limpid and open and our
ears wide awake.

These stories preferred over the ones
printed on our class teacher's book page,
The ones they make us memorize in every
grade,
Preaching them as a gospel as true as
Teacher P's leather belt,
Ever itching to remind us of the colour of
our fate.

Columbus zipping like lightning across
our unprepared backs,
Ripping away our pride like cloth from our
Taino grandmama's loins,
While they're stuffing us full of timetables
and English people rhymes
to validate our existence,
But never telling us who our father truly is
Or giving us our inheritance.

Today, from my precarious perch beside the grassquits' nest,
I peruse the wretched mix of names from Hanover to Gallina Punta,
The possibilities of two months of summer,
The sugarcane and yam sticks, the potato slips,
The soldiered lines of pineapple fencing us in ,
My mother bent double coaxing the sexist soil to help her create our own history
from the remnants she could scrounge,
Her pride worn like a crown,
African princess landed on Jamaican shores.

Like first prize, I unwrap Cynicism born too early in a child with such bright eyes, and
It doesn't take me long to decide whose History I will rewrite.

And All I Do is Listen

I am quite satisfied to sit silently among
you and listen
to your important nonsensical drivel and
smile like the cynic that I am
as I so easily peel away the lies and nibble
at your truths.

At times like this I think to myself,
It is a beautiful thing when artists unite;

The writers with their keyboards or their
pens
The painters with their brushes and
finesse
The musicians with their strings and keys
and breath
The politicians with their tongues and not
much else.

It is a beautiful thing to see artists at their
best.

The Dream

The dream is to be
Or to become the smartest,
the fastest, the strongest,
the bravest, the greatest;
It is our bequest.
It's what makes us more than less.

The dream is to strive for the dream
House, car, job, woman, man,
To fulfill that perfectly ordained plan
Of another, merely mortal someone.

The dream is to live the dream to be seen,
to be known to have been,
Yet it would seem,
the dream to be supreme,

That dream is just out of reach.

Even the smartest,
the fastest, the strongest,
the bravest, the greatest,
Is still striving to attain it,
maintain it, retain it,

While others who will never embrace it
Still measure themselves by it
and at the end of it

Everyone is shapen or misshapen by the
dream.

Connected, yet disconnected,
Dissatisfied, disjointed,
We wrestle with, suppress each other
Not even understanding that
the dream was inherited unwittingly,
That we have become slaves
inside someone else's fantasy,

That we never (ever)
even caught a glimpse
of our own reality.

Chance Encounter on a Beach in Jamaica

I thought I knew why I came
Until I sat with you in the evening
Under the tree by the beach
And we shared our simplicities and our complexities.
We exposed ourselves to each other,
Two strangers on a bench by the shore of the Caribbean Sea.
The mosquitoes were out to make their mark
And the waves competed for our attention
But it was the simple honest conversation
That is best between strangers
That lingers now.
Thanks to you, my new friend.

For you, Kristen.

In my chest, in the little cozy space between my breasts,

I have laid straw and soft things and made a nest,
A secure haven for my babies' heads to rest.

I carried them there when they were just a thought playing in my head
I've carried them there from that first moment, that first breath
To that first step, and that first spill
While I gather up a million prayers at will
And sing them the songs my mother used to sing.

I carry their weight there like I carry their bags in the mornings when we go to meet the taxi at the gate,
Like I carried their this and that from last night when we played.
I carry them there on days when they are not quite well
On anxious days when I have to wait for a doctor to tell;

On days when the questions are more than the answers I can give,
On those days when they're the sole reason why I live.

Some day when their wings have grown strong enough to fly
When they leave the haven to give their own space a try
I'll carry fond memories, I'll carry them in my prayers
I'll carry them forever in that little nest
That cozy place between my breasts,
Where I laid my heart for their heads to rest,
I'll carry my Loves right there on my chest.

Sonnet of Love

These ageless words like birds extend
their wings
To traipse o'er race and creed and
ceaseless time
Their light feet dance for starvelings and
for kings
Melodic voices lilt in perfect rhyme.

These ageless words from sacred pulpit
thrown
To wash the guilt from man's e'er flailing
soul
Like feckless leaves on fickle storm winds
blown
Yet sure as sextons rising for the toll.

I've seen them fill the cupboards of the
poor
In direst need help sick or weary cope
I've seen them lighten death's despairing
door
Touch hearts and minds with healing
hands of hope.

From thence till now there's nothing that can do
The wonders of these three word– I love you.

Silly Season

I don't remember when my heart began to
beat and skip and leap
and dance around in circles
but if I calculate, maybe not the exact date
it would be just about the time that I met
you
and you started smiling at me when there
was no joke
and your voice became whisper soft the
moment I came around.
When you pushed through the sneering
crowd just to hold my hand
and my every little whim or wish became
your command
and you said silly things to make me feel
at ease
and we had a song;
and you didn't want anyone else's eyes to
touch me too hard or too long
and we could sip from the same cup
without a second thought
and when we held hands the world
stopped and restarted at a run and

everything else became pale and
insignificant.
Your eyes would light up when I came
along
and my name was always at the tip of your
tongue
and I could never remember where you
ended and where I began but I think of it
now as that silly season
when our love was born.

For my sisters and my nieces, and all my other sisters,
I see you! Also for my beautiful country, I see you!

Metamorphosis

To the little girl inside me
Curled up ever so neatly in a corner of
yourself
Quietly listening to everything and
everybody else
Patiently painting pictures of blue skies
dotted with yellow butterflies
Basking in the perfumed smell of peach
roses from your imagination
Or from across the neighbour's fence,
I see you, I hear you even though you
never said
The things you wish you had and could
The things you want to, but you always do
the things you should.

I hear the whispers of your heartbeat,
See your timid feet dance in perfect time
Across every dividing line that holds you
in
I feel the rush of wind upon your skin
The wind of change you long for,
Dream about in sleepless nights.

I feel the pinch of disappointment,
The poke, the jab, the cruel knife
The elbow in the throat of your existence,
The claustrophobic pressure of the box
that keeps you in.
I see the ropes that firmly hold your hands
behind you,
See the sting of loss, the scratch, the tear,
Tattooed memories of the horrors you
were forced to bear.

I hear the screeching of the darkness,
See you step outside its will,
I see you hold the light you crafted,
Feel you raise the dreams you spilled.

To the little girl inside me,
Unfolding ever so neatly from the corner
inside yourself,
I see the beauty of your metamorphosis,
I hear your soft wings,
I feel your warm sunshine, I see you fly,
Beautiful yellow butterfly.

My Story

I live, I love, I feel,
I write and sometimes I speak.
From the depth of my humanness,
I am able to pour out a teensy bit of what I
hope is love and goodness.

I have had many experiences and maybe
many more encounters
which have dragged me along and left me
in a different place from where they found
me.
I have found that it is not those that cost
me more in dollars and cents
but in fact those which have cost me more
of myself
and at the end of it have left me with the
little dregs of wisdom
at the very bottom of my cup of knowledge
that have made the most sense, and it is
those that I appreciate the most and wish
to share with you my friends.

I live to love, to feel, to hope, to dream,
and when I speak it is through a
selectively permeable sieve which holds
back most of the knowledge and lets
through as much of the dregs as possible
and although some may choke on it,
others will tolerate it quite well and will
recognize it for what it is and will embrace
it like true friends
and then I'll know that that stories that I
told
Were really mine to tell.

Becoming

There is something that makes each of us unique. It's not our looks or mannerisms, usually those can be duplicated. It goes way deeper than that, to our very core. There's a need in each of us to be seen and felt in a particular way and I believe it is that need that distinguishes us from others.

The trouble is, too many of us, for one reason or another, never get to express our uniqueness. We are born into a world that has already prescribed our journey. Our path is preordained and I think most of us just go where we are led.

However, some of us dare to look out the window and to formulate our own dreams and we realize that we have something inside of us that doesn't quite sound like what the teacher just said. That something is desire. It's a longing to be. In my experience, that desire is usually encapsulated in a set of innate skills that is perfect for one's development.

That desire is a key that can unlock a thousand doors and open up a million dreams but we have to first acknowledge it. We then have to accept it for what it is. We have to own it, be proud of it and do everything we can to enhance and promote it. Then we have to understand that opposition will come and when it does, we have to stand our ground. Each of us is born to become someone who will, over time and in a particular space, enrich our generation and the next and when we understand and embrace that, that is ***becoming***.

I Am Here!

Who am I?
Where did I come from?
Who decided that I should be created,
that I should be
A woman?

Who envisioned this unique shape and
style
that is just so perfect for my dark brown
eyes?
Who kneaded and wielded and folded and
crafted
Then filled me with passion and pride?

I am the visual representation of an
imagination so complete,
So perfectly aligned with my every need.
There is nothing amiss,
I am stamped with the seal of perfection;
I am here, I am whole.
I am fearfully formed, wonderfully woven
Magnificently moulded into a unique and
beautiful soul!

Acknowledgements

Thanks to:

Rhys Bennett for photo editing and everything else plus his unwavering support.

Kyle Bennett for believing this dream.

Marcia and Garrina Clarke for always being there even when they didn't even realize they were a part of the dream.

Glo and Lor.

Made in the USA
Columbia, SC
20 December 2024

50188264R00050